THE LIFE OF PRAYER

THE
LIFE OF PRAYER

BY

BARON FRIEDRICH von HÜGEL

WIPF & STOCK · Eugene, Oregon

Wipf and Stock Publishers
199 W 8th Ave, Suite 3
Eugene, OR 97401

The Life of Prayer
By von Hügel, Baron F, LLD
ISBN 13: 978-1-60608-384-0
Publication date 12/30/2008
Previously published by E. P. Dutton & Co., 1929

The two following addresses were delivered by Baron von Hügel at Beaconsfield on 26 October and 27 October, 1921, and were published in the Second Series of his "Essays and Addresses on the Philosophy of Religion." They are here re-issued in a separate form in the belief that they will appeal to a wider circle of readers. It has been well said that "the essence of actual religion lay for Friedrich von Hügel in heroic virtue and in adoration." These addresses are perhaps the pages in his works that should prove most helpful in guiding souls along the way of the spiritual life on which he himself was one of the most shining lights in our times.

THE EDITOR.

THE LIFE OF PRAYER

I

THE FACTS AND DOCTRINES CONCERNING GOD WHICH ARE OF ESPECIAL IMPORTANCE IN THE LIFE OF PRAYER

I FIND IT IMPOSSIBLE TO restrict myself here to explicit tests of Scripture or to the Dogmatic Definitions of the Christian Faith. On the other hand, I will only put forward certain positions which have behind them large affirmations or assured implications of Scripture and great Fathers and theologians of the Church—positions which, if, in recent centuries or in our own times, largely ignored or explained away, nevertheless express the never extinct Christian and Catholic experience. Working within these lines and drawing also upon my own fifty years of endeavour in these matters, I find the positions concerning God, which require full and intelligent adoption in our life of Prayer, to be seven.

I

God is a stupendously rich Reality—the alone boundlessly rich Reality. His outward action throughout the Universe—His creation, sustentation and direction of the world at large—is immensely rich. Still deeper and more delicate is this richness and reality in God's Incarnation and Redemptive Action. Yet His Being, His Interior Life, are in no wise exhausted by all this outward Action, nor does this action occasion or articulate His character. We indeed, we little mortals—they too, the greatest of angels—we become our true selves, we articulate our spiritual characters, by apprehending, willing and serving God. But God is God, already apart from His occupation with us. These are the great facts which I believe to be specially revealed to us in the dogma of the Holy Trinity—facts of which we have an especial need in these our times. The whole of the Negative Theology, where it is sound and not really agnostic or pantheistic, is but an attempt to utter vividly this stupendous richness of God.

Our prayer will lack the deepest awe and widest expansion, if we do not find room within it for this fact concerning God. We will thus retain a strong sense that not even Jesus Christ and His Redemption exhaust God. Christian prayer, indeed Christian theology, are thus not Soteriology, practical or theoretical. Here Fénelon's great letters to the Carmelite nun, Sœur Charlotte de S. Cyprien, are admirable in their tender devotion to Christ free from all excessive Christocentrism.

2

God is the author of, and God is variously reflected in, all (innocent) Nature as well as in all Supernature. Here is the doctrine which was central in the outlook of Aquinas and Dante, of St. Francis and of Giotto. It was very largely forgotten or denied afterwards, during the later Middle Ages. And, although the Renaissance and then the Protestant Reformation were (variously wise and wild) protests against the abuses of the later Middle Ages, these movements were themselves largely infected by the impoverished philosophy and the thin theology of these same later Middle Ages. The signs are multiplying that man will return, with such improvements as may be wisely desirable, to that wonderfully rich outlook of the

Golden Middle Ages, where God's outward action moves on two levels—the natural level and the supernatural level—a Good and a Better or Best—two *kinds,* and not merely two degrees, of Goodness. *We thus recognise in man's actual life a polarity, a tension, a friction, a one thing at work in distinctly another thing*—like yeast in meal, like salt in meat, like coral insects and whole coral reefs in the huge ocean—an ocean so different from themselves. We thus also acquire an explanation, and one which is not discouraging, of the fact that it is a difficult art to prevent religion from overstraining us and from thus leading to a very dangerous reaction against itself. For thus we see that the Beatitude of Heaven—the Direct Vision of God, that the sincere forgiveness of our enemies, the love of them, and that the eager acceptance of suffering, are graces and dispositions beyond, and different from, God apprehended as the dim background or groundwork of our lives, and from the honesties and decencies of average domestic and political life. Such honesties and decencies are also good, and they are necessary for us all, in various degrees and forms; and this, also, as the occasions and material for the supernatural to utilise and transform —the Mountain and the Plain, the Edelweiss, and Alpenrose, and the cornfields and potatoes; here all appear, and this in fruitful contrast and congenital inter-aid.

Such an inclusive and yet discriminating position brings also much help to our prayer. For in prayer, also, it brings a tension, to the verge of strain; and a *détente,* to the verge of relaxation. In both these movements of the soul God can, and God should, be envisaged—in the *détente,* the God of nature, the source of all that is wholesome and homely; and in the tension, the God of supernature, the source of all that is ardent and heroic. We thus escape dullness, monotony and the like—these subtle dangers of the spiritual life.

3

God alone is fully free. Here is another ancient doctrine which calls aloud for resuscitation. It is already clearly formulated by St. Augustine, and Aquinas elaborates it in its fullness. But the later Middle Ages largely lost it, and Protestants to this hour have, in this point, merely extended and hardened the later Mediæval obtuseness. Indeed, even the present Broad High Churchmen of the type of *Foundations* have, for the most part, elaborated an apologetic with regard to the dread fact of Evil which deliberately eliminates the great doctrine here envisaged. St. Augustine tells us: "*It is already a great freedom to be able not to sin. But the greatest freedom consists in the inability to sin.*" And Aquinas elaborates how

Perfect Freedom consists in the spontaneous and joyous self-expression of a perfect nature. Thus God cannot will, God possesses no inclination to, Evil; and this absence of choice springs from precisely the perfection of His Freedom.

The persistent and vivid apprehension of this fact will greatly help our prayer. For thus only are we adequately humbled before God, since the difference between God and man is thus, essentially, not a difference, however great, in performance but in *nature*. Far beyond the range of our actual sinfulness extends the range of our potential sinfulness—of the imperfection inherent in our human degree and kind of Freedom. Whereas God is not only not actually sinful at all—He is incapable of sin, incapable of temptation to sin.

But there exists, not only God Pure, but also God Incarnate, Jesus Christ. Here, again, there is no actual sinfulness, and here also the sinlessness is a most wholesome occasion of humility to ourselves, the manifoldly sinful. In Jesus Christ the closeness of the union of His human nature with the Divine nature—with a Divine Person—renders actual sin impossible even in that Human nature. Nevertheless this human nature in itself is, even here, not above real temptation. "He was in all points tempted as we are, yet without sin," says the Epistle to the Hebrews (iv. 15). Here, again, it is important for us to understand that even such temptation—temptation without sin—is an imperfection pertaining to a certain kind of freedom—to the human kind of freedom—and not a necessary condition of all freedom, of freedom as such. For thus in Prayer we can, we will, look up to, adore God, the Perfect Freedom, which contrasts so grandly with our own poor little freedom

—even with our freedom where this exists in us, and is used by us, at its very best.

4

God is the Supreme Good—of the stone and of the plant, of the animal, of man, of the angel, but in what wondrously various degrees both of self-communication on the part of God, and of consciousness on the part of the creature, as to this gift from God, and still more as to the Giver, God Himself! In proportion to the depth and the breadth of any and every creature's nature, the creature possesses, or can attain to, the consciousness that God is its sole ultimate rest, sole pure delight. Religion, as distinct from ethics, flies straight at once to this great ultimate fact, to this unique personalist reality, to God as Beatitude and Beatifier. Thus the religious soul, in proportion to the strength of its religion, always reaches beyond all abstract law, all mere sense of duty and of obligation. St. Augustine is the great doctor of this our divine rest and our divine delight.

Our prayer will be immensely enriched and expanded by a persistent cultivation of this sense of God as our true home. For thus the rivalry between God and creatures for the possession of our hearts will become less and less a struggle between a mysterious obligation and a clear fascination, and more and more a competition between an ocean-wide, all-penetrating joy, when our souls come to their true, deep selves, and pleasures feverish, fleeting and shallow, when we allow ourselves heedlessly to be carried along by our superficial selves.

5

God, we have thus already found, is, indeed, not all unlike man. For how, if God were all unlike him, could man apprehend

God, and love God, and try "to be perfect even as our heavenly Father is perfect"? Yet God is also *other than man.* Other, because He, God, is a Reality, an Identity, a Consciousness, distinct from the reality, identity, consciousness of any of His creatures or of the sum-total of them. And God is other, because this His distinct Reality is, by its nature, so much higher and richer, not only in degree but in kind, than is the nature of man or of any other creature. "Man is made in the image and likeness of God." Yes, but we must not press this as an exhaustive norm, as though God were simply man writ large—man's better and best instincts and conditions on an immense scale. We shall doubtless be much nearer the facts if we think of God as the living Source and the always previous, always prevenient Realisation, in degrees and ways for us ineffable, of our ideals and ever imperfect achievements—a Realisation which must not be taken directly to contain concretely what our conditions and strivings contain ideally. I am deeply convinced that the truth, and hence the fascination of Religion, as really requires some such emphasis on the *unlikeness* of God as it requires emphasis upon the likeness. So, for instance, "God is Love" is a central truth proclaimed by the New Testament and by all the saints of God. And so again, "God careth for us"—that God is full of sympathy for all His creatures, and for man especially, Jesus Himself never ceases to proclaim and to illustrate. Yet we must beware not to press this further, so as to mean suffering in God. For suffering is an evil, and there exists no evil in God: the religious instinct spontaneously and unchangeably hungers after God as Pure Joy. With St. Bernard, in his classic lament on the death of his darling twin-brother Gerard, we will hold that there exists the deepest *compassio,* but no *passio* in God.

Yet our hearts long also (though less strongly, I believe) for downright fellow-suffering, when they suffer and when they are exhorted to suffer well. Such fellow-suffering (deeper than ever we ourselves could suffer, and in One Who shares with us the evil of suffering, but without any admixture of the far greater evil of sin) is supplied by the Humanity of Our Lord. The Humanity of Jesus Christ, we have already found, brings temptation as near to God as is compatible with Godhead. And now we find this same Humanity of Jesus brings suffering as near to God as is compatible with the same Godhead. Indeed, the sufferings are so great as to require, for their sustainment by His human nature, the presence and action of the Divine nature, of the Divine Person which has conjoined itself to, and which informs, this human nature.

Our prayer will profit greatly if we thus hold firmly and fervently this double truth:

of the *Pure Joy of God and of the Deep Suffering of Jesus.* For we will thus neither diminish God to a man of but larger size than we little men are, nor will we dehumanise Jesus by ignoring the immense sufferings, as well as the storm and stress—the temptations—of His earthly life. The definition of the Council of Chalcedon, difficult as it may be to apply it in any great detail, will thus continue to enshrine for us, also as praying souls, an imperishable truth: Jesus Christ is both truly God and truly Man.

6

All we have so far said implies or leads up to the great fact and truth: that *we men need God much more than, and very differently from, the way and degree in which God needs us men.* God is the Absolute Cause, the Ultimate Reason, the Sole True End and Determiner of our existence, of our persistence, of our nature, of our essential calls and requirements. God is all these things for man. Man is not one of these things for God. Man comes to his true self by loving God. God is the very ocean of Himself—of Love—apart from all creation. Thus the positions between God and Man, and between Man and God, are entirely uninterchangeable. Hence the most fundamental need, duty, honour and happiness of man, is not petition, nor even contrition, nor again even thanksgiving; these three kinds of prayer which, indeed, must never disappear out of our spiritual lives; but *adoration.* Probably the greatest doctor and the greatest practiser among souls well known to us in these respects, of such overwhelmingly adoring prayer, is St. Augustine. Never, in spite of his tenderly anthropomorphic devotion, does the great African forget this profound non-equality, this non-interchangeable relation between God and man. Our prayer will greatly deepen and widen out, if we also develop such a sense—a sense which is now continually exposed to the subtle testing and sapping of the pure immanentisms and the sentimental anthropocentrisms which fill the air.

7

The Prevenience of God thus appears as the root-fact and the root-truth of all our previous positions. God not only loves us more and better than we can ever love ourselves, "*carior est illis*"—to the Gods—"*homo quam sibi,*" already Juvenal told us; but God loved us before we loved, or could love, Him. God's love of us rendered possible and actual our love of God. This is emphatically proclaimed by the First Epistle of St. John, and is a favourite doctrine of St. Bernard. Thus the great Cistercian Abbot bids his monks rise never so early for their night choir prayer in coldest mid-winter; they will find God awake, Him the awakener; they will find Him waiting for them, always anticipating even their earliest watches. How scandalously much is this great fact forgotten in our days, even by otherwise alert preachers to educated congregations! I had much talk with an Australian nonconformist minister upon this point, some ten years ago; and he determined to preach it before such a congregation—a large one in London. He afterwards reported to me that his discourse had made a great stir, crowds of his hearers flocking into the vestry to declare to him that they never in their lives had heard such doctrine, and how wonderful and awakening it was!

Our prayer will certainly gain in depth and aliveness, if we thus continually think of God as the true inspirer of our most original-seeming thoughts and wishes, whensoever these are good and fruitful—as Him Who secretly initiates what He openly crowns.

I take these to be the seven great facts and doctrines concerning God—His richness, His double action, natural and supernatural, His perfect Freedom, His delightfulness, His otherness, His adorableness and His prevenience. These seven facts, vividly apprehended, will even singly and how much more if seen conjointly, each penetrating and calling forth the others, bring much depth and breadth, much variety and elasticity into our prayer. This, however, only if we understand plainly that there is no occasion whatsoever for us to constrain ourselves *positively* on these points. I mean that, though a Christian's prayer will suffer in its Christianity, if it consciously and systematically excludes, still more if it denies, any of these facts, yet no one soul, at any one period of its spiritual life, will feel equally attracted to them all. It will be quite enough—indeed it will be the only wise course—if each particular soul, at any one period of its growth, attends positively, affirmatively, and lovingly to two or three, or even to but one of these facts. Thus not any one soul, but the society of souls, the Church of Christ, will simultaneously apprehend and apply all these facts and truths. The Church's several constituents and organs will supplement each other, and will, collectively, furnish a full perception and a full practice of these great facts of God.

II

THE FACTS AND TRUTHS CONCERNING THE SOUL WHICH ARE OF MOST IMPORTANCE IN THE LIFE OF PRAYER

MUCH IN HUMAN PSYCHOLOGY and epistemology has been rendered more clear during the last thirty years or so, and some very ancient misconceptions have now been finally cleared up. Yet the presentation and the penetration of the processes operative in the life of prayer, which we owe to a St. Augustine, a St. Bernard, a St. Teresa, remain unsurpassed, indeed, on the central points, unapproached to this very hour. I take the points which concern the human mind and spirit, indeed man's complex organism generally, in so far as they come largely into play in the life of prayer, to be again seven. The due allocation and utilisation of the seven psychological facts and laws will, very largely, depend upon the degree to which we have adequately and vividly apprehended the seven great facts and truths concerning God. Indeed, a certain amount of overlapping and repetition is unavoidable as between the two series of facts, where each set of facts is, doubtless, in itself, very distinct from the other set, yet where the one set has to be apprehended by, and has to be put into close relation with, the other set.

I

The decisive preparation for prayer lies not in the prayer itself, but in the life prior to the prayer. That is, distractions and dryness, indeed even the real fruitlessness in and of our prayer, spring largely from our faulty dispositions, doings and driftings when out of prayer. The effects of such faultinesses pursue us when we come to pray. The cure for such faults committed out of prayer, and for their effects upon and within prayer, lies in the very wise ordering, and in the very faithful execution of such ordering, of our active life.

Fénelon pointed out to the Duc de Chevreuse how overburdened, and how racketed and distracted was the Duke's life, outside of his direct and deliberate praying; and how greatly that over-burdenedness, when out of prayer, damaged his recollection when in prayer. Fénelon advised the Duke to begin his day with quietly running through in his mind the chief things he would probably have to do, or would probably be solicited to do, during that coming day. That he should then and there reduce the number of such things as much as was wisely possible. And that, when he came to the actual doing of these things, he should clip his action of all unnecessary detail and development. *In this way he would succeed in placing each action within a circumambient air of leisure—of leisure for the spirit of prayer and peace.* This would be like the ordering of a wise gardener, who carefully sees to it that the young trees he plants have sufficient spaces each from the other—have sufficient air in which to grow and expand. I have myself greatly profited by striving to practise this advice.

St. Catherine of Genoa's method of life has also helped me much. She would quietly concentrate, each moment, upon that moment's special content—upon God's gift and will of special suffering or joy, of determination, effort, decision and the like, conveyed within that moment. Such a scheme follows out something similar, within the spiritual life, to the action of the sun upon the sundial in physical life. The sun successively touches and illumines this, and then that, and then the next radius of the dial. Or, again, the scheme reminds one of Goethe's old mother, Frau Rath, who, when one day an acquaintance, ignorant of Frau Rath's condition, called at her door and asked to see her, sent down a message to the visitor that "Frau Rath was busy dying." Indeed, a genial, quiet death to self lies in every minute, when the minute is thus taken separately as the dear will and the direct vehicle of God.

2

The ceaseless interdependence of Soul and Body. The more any state of soul—any *psychosis*—is mental, still more is spiritual, or at least the more the agent or patient feels the *psychosis* to be thus mental or spiritual, the less, as a rule, is the neural accompaniment, the neural limitation, and the neural cost of this state perceived at the time by the experiencing soul. Yet such accompaniment, limitation and cost are certainly present, even in the most genuine and highest of man's spiritual actions or states; indeed, the neural cost appears, roughly, to rise in proportion as the action, at the time, fails to bring with it any sense of cost at all.

Fénelon is admirably awake to this important fact, when he warns Madame de Montberon not to indulge, beyond a certain limited time, in the prayer of quiet—a prayer which greatly helped and refreshed her; and this because of the neural cost of such effortless-seeming prayer.

One quite general, yet very helpful preparation towards the practice of sobriety in prayer, and hence towards escaping, as far as possible, the acute reactions liable to follow upon such very delightful prayer, is admirably preached and practised by Jean Nicholas Grou. This fine classical scholar, and deeply spiritual writer and leader of souls, urges *the importance of the soul's possession and cultivation of two levels and kinds of action and interest*—a wholesome natural interest and action, and a deep supernatural interest and action. The soul will then possess and will cultivate a genuine interest in politics or economics, in language or history, in natural science or philosophy—in these, as part of its bread-winning or as quite freely chosen studies. And we will thus, when in dryness and even in anticipation of it, possess a most useful range of interest to which to turn, as our disporting ground, in relief of the dreariness or the strain of our directly religious life. I believe Grou's spiritual writings remain so fresh, because (given his spiritual experience) he never, as he tells us himself, wrote on religious subjects except when the spiritual light and fervour were within him; whilst at other—the far more frequent—times he translated Plato or emended the texts of Livy and Horace.

Some further hints towards the bearing and the utilisation of desolation, as part and parcel of every at all religious life, and of every at all complete self-knowledge possessed by the liver of such a life. Thus St. Teresa, especially in her Autobiography, gives us admirably vivid descriptions of her times of dryness. On the other hand, I was surprised and disappointed when, some fifteen months ago, that deeply sincere Indian convert, the Sadhu Sundar Singh, told me that, never since his conversion thirteen years before, had he ever suffered one moment of spiritual dryness. I believe, with a very experienced psychologist and philosopher friend of mine, that this opinion indicates a strange lack of self-knowledge, perhaps also of what is precisely meant by such dryness, on the part of this devoted Christian. If, then, spiritual dryness is indeed inevitable in the life of prayer, we will be much helped to bear these desert stretches, by persistent recognition—hence also, indeed especially, in our times of fervour—of the normality and the necessity of such desolation. We will thus come to treat desolation in religion as we treat the recurrence of the night within every twenty-four hours of our physical existence; or as bodily weariness at the end of any protracted exertion in our psychic life. When desolation is actually upon us, we will quietly modify, as far as need be, the kind and the amount of our prayer—back, say, from prayer of quiet to ordinary meditation, or to vocal prayer—even to but a few uttered aspirations. And, if the desolation is more acute, we will act somewhat like the Arab caravans behave in the face of a blinding sandstorm in the desert. The men dismount, throw themselves upon their faces in the sand; and there they remain, patient and uncomplaining, till the storm passes, and until, with their wonted patient endurance, they can and do continue on their way.

There are generally a weakness and an error at work within us, at such times, which considerably prolong the trouble, and largely neutralise the growth this very trouble would otherwise bring to our souls. The weakness lies in that we let our imagination and sensitiveness be directly absorbed in our trouble. We contemplate, and further enlarge, the trouble present in ourselves, instead of firmly and faithfully looking away, either at the great abiding realities of the spiritual world, or, if this is momentarily impossible for us, at some other, natural or human, wholesome fact or law. And the error lies in our lurking suspicions that, for such trials to purify us, we must feel them fully in their tryingness—that is, we must face and fathom them directly and completely. Such a view completely overlooks the fact that such trials are sent us for the purpose of deoccupying us with our smaller selves; and, again, it ignores the experience of God's saints across the ages, that, precisely in proportion as we can get away from direct occupation with our troubles to the thought and love of God, to the presence of Him Who permits all this, in the same proportion do and will these trials purify our souls.

3

The great difference, in spiritual range and depth, in special *attrait* and peculiar calls and gifts, *unchangeably inherent in each soul's vocation to what it is, and still more to what God would have it become.* True, certain differences, perceptible on the surface, between soul and soul, largely spring from some changeable causes or defects. And, again, at the opposite end, the ultimate limitations as well as the possible final calls of individual souls are completely known to God alone, and to the soul itself, with some real knowledge, only and when it has advanced considerably on the spiritual way. Still, even the soul which is but a beginner can, with a little reflection and some good advice, save itself either much unnecessary failure, or, again, much vagueness and superficiality of endeavour, if it sorts out, roughly and for practical purposes, those acts, habits, intentions, self-conquests, etc., which specially appeal to it in its deepest, most peaceful moments, or which are specially called for by its particular character in the peculiar circumstances of its life and call: if it fixes upon *these* dispositions and virtues, and makes *these* things the central objects of its prayers and endeavours. It will work at these things—at least for a while—on a relatively wide and deep scale, and, as to the other virtues and dispositions, it will be content with not completely neglecting them. If we are faithful and humble in this concentration and cultivation, we shall come to discover any serious mistakes we may have made in our original choice, and we can then correspondingly widen, or narrow, or shift, the field, or alter the methods of our operations.

All this directly concerns our prayer also. For all such choosing of the field of our spiritual self-cultivation, all our labours in this field, all our little successes, many failures, and long awaitings of *some* fruit: all this should be *saturated with prayer*—by the spirit of prayer and by definite prayer, vocal, mental or of quiet. And, again, these several kinds of prayer, or combinations of kinds: these too, of course, should be chosen with due care and circumspection, according, again, to the *attrait,* the need, and the experience of the particular soul, which, however, must never be allowed to eliminate all vocal prayer.

Bishop Creighton wrote a fine letter, given in his *Life,* on the wonderfully rich variety which characterised the spiritual life of the Mediæval Church at its best; and, indeed, such varieties continue to flourish in the Roman Catholic Church. When Frederick William Faber preached the panegyric of St. Ignatius Loyola, on the occasion of the Feast of the Founder of the Jesuits, in the Jesuit church at Farm Street, he spent an hour in unbroken, sympathetic, indeed fervent, exposition of this saint's spirituality, and only in his last sentence did he introduce the necessary limitation and expansion: "This, then, my dear brethren, is St. Ignatius's way to heaven; and, thank God, it is not the only way!"

A friend of mine, who loved her garden, told me how only one of the many gardeners employed by her had succeeded with every one of her roses. She asked him what was the secret of his success. He told her that the other gardeners treated all her roses, not unwisely, but too generally—they treated them all in precisely the same way; whereas he himself watched across the months each rose-bush separately, and followed out, for each plant, that plant's special *attrait* as to soil, manure, sun, air, water, support, shelter and the like. So with souls: let us, without undue self-occupation, learn to discriminate between them and, again, between them all and ourselves, so as both to respect and encourage *their* ways, however different from our own, and to persevere and improve in *our* ways, however lonely these ways may be.

4

The Incarnational side of religion may never be despised nor forgotten, but must always be assigned *some* definite place and power within our spiritual lives. The approach to God and the condescension of God, the Invisible, Pure Spirit, on occasion of, in, and with the Sensible and Visible—the Historical, Traditional, Social, Sacramental—must remain and be cultivated within our souls.

The fact is that Pure Mysticism is but Pantheism; and that Pantheism is, on principle and incurably, a non-moral, a supra-moral and a non-personalist position, within which there is really no place for a distinct and definite God, for Sin, for Contrition, for the sense of our being creatures, and for Adoration. All attempts to interpret the whole life and teaching of Jesus, as simply the supreme unfolding of Pure Mysticism, suffer shipwreck against the great convictions which colour all the words and deeds of Jesus, that the consummation is indeed proximate, but not present; that its beginnings can indeed already be seen, but not its fulfilment; and that even these beginnings, and still more the fulfilment, are the deed of God, the immensely Personalist Power, and not the work of mankind, still less just the operation of the world-whole. The supreme revelation of the omni-present, non-successive God, took place, in unique fashion and degree, in such and such years, and months and days and hours, and in such and such places, of human history. And so, similarly, with His lesser, yet still real, self-communications.

Now there is no doubt that *the prayer of quiet*—that *a certain formless recollection and loving feeding upon the sense and presence of God*—of God, as here and now—is a most legitimate prayer. Indeed, for the souls which possess the call to, and capacity for, such prayer (and their number is, I believe, not so very small), this form of prayer will feed and fortify their spirit more than would, *at the times when such prayer can healthily operate,* any number of vocal prayers, formal meditations, or Church services. Nevertheless—and this is our present special point—such prayer of quiet will remain safe and wholesome only if *some* daily vocal prayers, and *some* more or less frequent Church attendances and sacramental acts and receptions, continue active within this same soul's life. I know well that such sensible and spiritual practices will, to such a soul, bring with them, at least at their beginnings, a feeling of incongruity, of oppression, of contraction, sometimes only dull, but at other times very acute. Yet every such initial discomfort, if only the sensible-spiritual acts be chosen with reasonable reference to this soul's special call, and if these acts be bravely faced and persevered in, will (if not promptly, at least in the long run) be followed by an increase, very real, and mostly also clearly perceived, of the substantiality, and of humble, childlike quality in the prayer of quiet, and in the entire character of this same soul.

Let me illustrate what I mean from my own direct experience. After practising a daily three-point meditation for some twenty-five years, the new Helper sent me by God advised me that my prayer should now be mainly informal—more of the prayer of quiet type; but that there should always remain short vocal prayers morning and night, Mass and Holy Communion twice a week, with Confession once a week or once a fortnight; and (perhaps most characteristic point of all) one decade of the rosary every day—this especially to help prevent my interior life from losing touch with the devotion of the people. After over thirty years of this mixed *régime,* I am profoundly convinced of the penetrating sagacity of this advice.

Let me, then, suggest that we should each

of us discover, with sufficient detail, what is the form of prayer to which God appears to call us; let us give ample room and opportunity to this particular form; but let us also organize, most carefully, a certain regular amount of the other kinds of prayer and worship.

5

The right attitude towards the Sex-instinct, and as to what is, for the Christian, the sin of sins.

Original Sin was generally considered by Catholic Christians, up to the advent of the great Jesuit theologians, as a *stain,* a vicious habit present within human souls from the moment of their conception and birth into this earthly life. And especially St. Augustine, following and still further accentuating the attitude of St. Paul, found this vicious habit to lie centrally in the vehemence of the sex-instinct. Not even St. Augustine dared censure the sex-instinct as such; as a Catholic Christian, he could not cast a slur upon marriage in its essentials. He declared a moderate, readily controllable sex-instinct to be right; only the vehemence, such as now characterises this instinct, was evil and part of original sin.

But the great Jesuit theologians found even this much to be untenable: how could an instinct, without which men would certainly not face the grave burdens of bringing dependent families into the world, be too strong, if we grant that the perpetuation of the human race really matters? So these Jesuit theologians placed the evil, not in the instinct, nor even in the vehemence of the instinct, but simply in the weakness of the reason and of the will called upon to control and moderate that vehemence.

Certain difficulties attach also to this view. Yet this view is satisfactory in that it removes all grounds for pains of conscience as to the presence of the sex-instinct, however strong this sex-instinct may be (apart, of course, from such strength as it may possess owing to the bad or slack life led by the soul which thus experiences the instinct).

Now I believe it to be of great importance that we should realise, vividly and persistently, that human purity is not only consistent with the presence of this instinct, but, at bottom, requires it. There doubtless can exist creatures of God without such an instinct. But man ceases to be human, unpossessed of such an instinct. Human purity is thus essentially a virtue operating within the body—a fleshly virtue.

Yet Mr. F. R. Tennant's books, so wholesomely suggestive on this point, should suffice to warn us how easily we can be led on to think of the body as ultimately the occasion of *all* our sins, as well as of our virtues; or, at least, to make impurity be, in our minds, *the* sin, the type and measure of all sin. For, with Tennant, *all* sin is but an *atavism,* a lapse back into the animalism from out of which mankind has raised itself. Impurity is a direct atavism—a gross, simple atavism, whilst *pride* is an indirect atavism—a subtilised, compound animalism. But this, I do not doubt, is a strangely inadequate view, both as to the sheer facts and as to the specifically Christian position. For the facts readily show that the occasions, the effects and the reactions of our consciousness with regard to Impurity, are all different from the occasions, the effects and the reactions of Pride. It is very distinctly *not* the animal within us which leads us to pride and self-sufficiency, whereas it is, quite as distinctly, the animal within us which does lead us to sloth, gluttony and impurity.

And as to the Christian outlook, its genius is sensitively keen and final concerning which is the central, the most heinous sin.

The central sin, for the Christian, is Pride and Self-sufficiency, distinctly more so than Impurity and Sloth.

I take the occasion, the very possibility of such pride and self-sufficiency, to spring, not from the body at all, but from the delicate poise of our imperfect freedom. We possess a real, but only partial independence; we own a limited power and a limited self-determinative freedom, and even these our fundamental qualities we owe, not to our own making or finding, but we hold them as gifts, as creations of God. The very deep doctrine of the Fall of the Angels grandly illustrates this position. The Angels are without bodies; yet this does not lift them above probation, but merely makes their testing a testing in Humility instead of Purity. And, again, this absence of bodies does not make the alternatives or the Fall of these Angels to be less. On the contrary, it makes them greater.

I can only say that these two convictions, as to the nature of human Purity, and as to the rank of Humility amongst the virtues of all the creatures of God, have greatly helped my prayer. For the conviction as to Purity has freed me from much previous scruple and depression: and the conviction as to Humility has, I feel, anchored me more deeply and more securely in the Christian Ideal, in the Christian life, and in the rich Christian fact—the life and spirit of Jesus Christ, Our Lord.

6

A right attitude towards Temptation and towards Sin. Such an attitude springs from two vivid perceptions: a keen sense of the difference between Perfect Liberty, as we found it to characterise God, and Imperfect Liberty, as it exists in man and, indeed, doubtless in all the higher and highest creatures of God; and an equally keen sense of how all-penetrating and all-characterising is, for man, the effect of this his Imperfect Liberty. The first sense, as to the Imperfection of our Liberty, will save us, as we have seen, from all pride, not only in our perhaps actually being some kind of Byron or Don Juan, but even in our ability thus to fall away from what we should be. And the second sense, as to the special character conferred upon all our moral and spiritual life by this our betwixt and between position of Imperfect Freedom, will keep us awake to the fact that, for our special human kind and degree of virtue, Temptation is indeed necessary, in the long run and upon the whole, for the perfecting and testing of our moral and spiritual life. Temptation—Temptation to sin—is necessary; but not the Commission of sin, not sin itself. Both these facts find their supreme illustration in the earthly life of Jesus. His Sinlessness

—the unquestioning conviction of His sinlessness—appears in the oldest documents, but also His Temptedness. This temptedness disappears already in the Fourth Gospel. Yet the Synoptic Gospels (especially St. Luke), and the Epistle to the Hebrews, give varied and quite unforced expression to the reality of these temptations and to the primitiveness of the belief in their reality. We thus secure the text: "He was tempted like unto ourselves in all points, yet without sin." This, for the Humanity even of Jesus Christ. And we affirm the doctrine "without Sin, without Temptation, without Suffering" —this, for God—indeed even for the divinity of Jesus Christ. "Credo in Deum Impassibilem," declared the Council of Aquileia.

I wish we could all vividly realise how all grave sin, actually committed by us, leaves —at least for and during this our earthly life—scars and limitations upon our souls, even after our most generous penitence. Thus St. Augustine did not simply profit by his sins. They became, indeed, the occasions for a grand humility and for the keenest sense of the mercy of God. He became, in spite of his past sins, a greater Saint than is many another saint whose sins were far fewer or far smaller. But Augustine the Sinner, even when he had become Augustine the Penitent, did not surpass, not even equal what—everything else being equal—would have been Augustine the Innocent. He would then, for instance, not have so closely grazed Gnosticism in his treatment of marriage. So, too, the noble founder of La Trappe, the vehement de Rancé, did not simply profit all round by his former sins, heroically repented of though they were. His aversion to all critical historical work, as part of the lives of monks, is doubtless an excess, and an excess which forms part of the reaction from his former worldly life. Here, too, the model of all models is Jesus Christ Our Lord —Jesus, and not even St. Paul. Our Lord's Humanity really grows and grows "in favour with God and man" amidst real temptation. But Jesus commits no sin; nor is there any trace of a reaction, still less of any excessive reaction, from a sinful life, or, indeed, from any single sin. And this Sinlessness does not spell weakness, but the fullest power.

Let us penetrate our prayer with these discriminations, and let us beware of loose thinking about the profitableness of sin, which, alas, even great poets such as Robert Browning have, at times, encouraged. I am very sure that, if we keep persistently awake to the contrast between ourselves, the tempted and sinning, and Jesus, the sinless but tempted, and again God, the living Reality beyond all sin and temptation, we shall greatly strengthen and fruitfully articulate our prayer.

7

The Divinely intended End of our Life is Joy overflowing and infinite, a Joy closely connected with a noble asceticism.

There is a wholesome, a strengthening *zest* attached to all action which is right and appropriate for the agent; and there is an unhealthily weakening *excitement,* which accompanies or follows all activity that is wrong or inappropriate. Hence one great end, and one sure test of right living and right dispositions, is the degree to which such living and dispositions make zest to prevail in our lives and make excitement to disappear from them. Now there is no zest comparable to the zest, the expansion, the joy brought to the soul by God and the soul's close union with Him. True, here below, we require to the end a filial reverence, fear, restraint; virtues which, in the beyond, will continue deepened, in the life of Adoration. True, again, we must never cease to fight Self, to flee from Self. "The love of God, even the contempt of self," must more and more supplant the "love of self, even to the contempt of God." We never may directly seek mere pleasure. Yet it is also true that we possess, deep within us, a spontaneous affinity for God. Nature draws us to God, as the dim, though most real background and groundwork of our existence; and Supernature raises this semi-conscious affinity to an active hunger for direct and clear vision, for a true participation in the Supernatural Life of God. Hence we must, in our practice, beware of deciding, as to what precisely to think, to do, to be, in execution of God's will for us, directly and simply in favour of what we do not like, or what we like least. We ought, instead, quietly to concentrate our thoughts upon God—upon His will and His various calls, and upon discovering which of such forms and degrees of moral and spiritual life most draws the soul in the moments of its greatest clearness and peacefulness, as to what is somehow meant for it. There will be plenty of opportunities for a large and deep asceticism within the life thus chosen, when we come, as assuredly we will, to have patiently to hold out, and laboriously to advance along the road—a road which, nevertheless, will be *the* road to Peace and to Power for the chooser.

We will not, of course, rule out, for ourselves or for others, the practice, or at least the spirit, also of bodily austerities. The spirit, and even some mild amount of the actual practice, of such austerities is, indeed, an integral constituent of all virile religion: the man who laughs at the plank bed and the discipline is a shallow fool. Indeed, some souls are, undoubtedly, called to more than the minimum indicated, and only find their full peace and persuasiveness in some such bodily asceticism. Thus there was a Sacred Heart nun, of whom I heard some time ago, who dearly loved, and anxiously watched over one of the pupils of the convent school, a beautiful young woman. This young woman, soon after leaving the school, took to an evil life and became a wealthy man's mistress. The nun knew well how unavailing would be, in this case, any direct appeal to the girl's religion or conscience. So she wrote to the girl that she was sure the girl loved her and wished her to live for many a year. Well, she merely wanted the girl to know that, on every day during which this her immoral life should last, she, the nun, would scourge herself till her feet stood in a pool of her own blood. That she had already carried out this plan daily since she knew of the girl's condition; and that nothing could or would stop her but the girl's own written announcement that she had left the man. The days went by. At last the girl wrote. The nun had gained her point. Is not that grand?

Yet it is Love, God, that first should be in our hearts; and if that Love then impels us to such deeds, we will attempt to do them, to feed and to express our love of that Love, and not otherwise. There is an admirable letter on asceticism generally from Fénelon to Madame de Maintenon. My own daughter, a Carmelite nun, spoke simply the spirit of her great Order, when, some little time ago, she answered an Anglican married lady, who declared herself repelled by all such mortifications—how could they ever form a part of the Christian life? Did not God Himself send us crosses, sufficient for all purposes, through and within our duties? Why arbitrarily add to these? The nun answered that she did not, indeed, find any trace of an *attrait* to such mortifications in her questioner—let her cheerfully leave such things alone and serve God joyfully along her way. That these things are never more than instruments or applications of the one spirit and way of love and of service. But that the lady would be unwise did she go further—if she condemned all such things for everyone. God's calls, within our one great common vocation, are many and various. Souls exist which are as truly called to such mortifications, as her soul was *not* called to them. Who are we, to lay down the law and the limit to God?

In either of these two paths, as Denifle draws out finely in his great Luther book, the general direction, the End and the Measure are the same—the love of God above all things and the love of our neighbour as ourselves. And this love of God, where uninhibited and full, brings Joy—it seeks God, Joy; and it finds Joy, God. I used to wonder, in my intercourse with John Henry Newman, how one so good, and who had made so many sacrifices to God, could be so depressing. And again, twenty years later, I used to marvel contrariwise, in my intercourse with the Abbé Huvelin, how one more melancholy in natural temperament than even Newman himself, and one physically ill in ways and degrees in which Newman never was, could so radiate spiritual joy and expansion as, in very truth, the Abbé did. I came to feel that Newman had never succeeded in surmounting his deeply predestinarian, Puritan, training; whilst Huvelin had nourished his soul, from boyhood upwards, on the Catholic spirituality as it flowered in St. Francis. Under the fine rule by which the Roman Church tribunals require, for Canonisation as distinct from Beatification, that the Servant of God concerned should be proved to have possessed and to have transmitted a deep spiritual joy, Newman, I felt and feel, could indeed be beatified, but only Huvelin could be canonised.

Our prayer will greatly benefit by the great facts and discriminations we have been considering. Without in any way forcing, or escaping from, our real *attrait,* our prayer will thus possess a double virile asceticism. We shall feel ourselves, even if personally not called to very definite or to large bodily mortifications, in spiritual touch with, and supplemented by, those who are; and, again, we will deliberately hold ourselves as pledged to much renunciation of facile pleasures, as the condition and cost of our own abiding Joy.

THE END

www.ingramcontent.com/pod-product-compliance
Lightning Source LLC
LaVergne TN
LVHW010543100826
845148LV00013B/2585

9781606083840